D0915940

Madam C.J. Walker

THE INSPRING LIFE STORY OF THE
HAIR CARE ENTREPRENEUR

BY DARLENE R. STILLE

COMPASS POINT BOOKS
a capstone imprint

Compass Point Books are published by Capstone,
1710 Roe Crest Drive, North Mankato, Minnesota 56003
www.mycapstone.com

Editorial Credits
Catherine Neitge and Angela Kaelberer, editors; Ashlee Suker, designer;
Wanda Winch, media researcher; Kathy McColley, production specialist

Photo Credits
A'Lelia Bundles/Madam Walker Family Collection, 4, 7, 8, 12, 19, 41, 45, 46,
54, 59, 72, 87, 88, 93, 97, 98, 101, 102, 103, 105, A'Lelia Bundles/Madam
Walker Family Collection/Sylvia Jones, 71, 76; The Annie Malone Children and
Family Services Center, St. Louis, Missouri, 29; Capstone, 52; The Denver Public
Library: Western History Collection, Photographer L.C. McClure, #MCC-4861,
39; Florida State Archives, 64, 99; Getty Images: Corbis/Bettmann, 83, Corbis/
George Rinhart, 91, Hulton Archive, 32, MPI, 79, The LIFE Picture Collection/
Wallace G. Levison , 22; Granger, NYC – All rights reserved, 10, 20, 25, 85;
Indiana Historical Society: Bass Photo Collection [209274-F], 67, Madam C.J.
Walker Collection [M0399-B2:F1 A69], 57, 104; Library of Congress: Manuscripts
Division, 34, Prints and Photographs Division, 15, 62, 69, 75, 81, 94; North
Wind Picture Archives: 17, 26, 51; The Schomburg Center for Research in Black
Culture: Prints Division/The New York Public Library/Astor, Lenox and Tilden
Foundation, 36;   Shutterstock: Ivgroznii, design element

Library of Congress Cataloging-in-Publication Data
Names: Stille, Darlene R., author.
Title: Madam C.J. Walker : the inspiring life story of the hair care
entrepreneur / by Darlene R. Stille.
Description: North Mankato, Minnesota : Compass Point Books, an imprint
of Capstone Press, [2017] | Series: CPB grades 4-8. Inspiring stories |
Includes bibliographical references and index.
Identifiers: LCCN 2016004334
ISBN 9780756551650 (library binding)
ISBN 9780756551872 (ebook pdf)
Subjects: LCSH: Walker, C. J., Madam, 1867-1919—Juvenile literature. |
African American women executives—Biography—Juvenile literature. |
Cosmetics industry—United States—History—Juvenile literature. | Women
millionaires—United States—Biography—Juvenile literature.
Classification: LCC HD9970.5.C672 S85 2017 | DDC 338.7/66855092—
dc23 LC record available at http://lccn.loc.gov/2016004334
LC record available at http://lccn.loc.gov/2016004334

Printed and bound in Canada.
009644F16

Table of Contents

CHAPTER ONE
FROM WASHERWOMAN TO MILLIONAIRE.........5

CHAPTER TWO
HUMBLE BEGINNINGS......................11

CHAPTER THREE
VICKSBURG LAUNDRESS....................21

CHAPTER FOUR
A NEW START IN ST. LOUIS................27

CHAPTER FIVE
A STEP TO A BETTER LIFE.................35

CHAPTER SIX
SPREADING THE WORD.....................47

CHAPTER SEVEN
A NEW HOME AND FACTORY.................55

CHAPTER EIGHT
EARNING RESPECT........................63

CHAPTER NINE
FACING DISCRIMINATION..................77

CHAPTER TEN
LATER YEARS............................89

TIMELINE...............................102
GLOSSARY...............................106
ADDITIONAL RESOURCES...................107
SOURCE NOTES...........................108
SELECT BIBLIOGRAPHY....................110
INDEX..................................111
CRITICAL THINKING USING THE COMMON CORE...........112

Madam C. J. Walker made millions of dollars and furthered the cause of civil rights.

Chapter One

FROM
WASHERWOMAN
TO MILLIONAIRE

*S*arah Breedlove McWilliams Davis stared at her reflection in the mirror and frowned. She was about to have her photograph taken, and she wasn't happy about how she looked. She was just 26 years old, but her hair was extremely damaged and falling out rapidly. Sarah tried to style her hair to look nice for the photo, but all she could do was smooth down the sides a bit and form the hair near her face into short, frizzy bangs. Sarah worried that, before long, she would be completely bald.

Davis wasn't the only African-American woman in the 1890s to experience problems with her hair. At the time most people believed regular shampooing wasn't good for the hair. Many washed their hair only once a month or even less often in the winter. Unwashed scalps can develop severe dandruff caused by flakes of dead skin. Davis' job as a laundress didn't help her hair problems either. As she washed clothes and bedding by hand in washtubs, the steaming hot water made her scalp sweat and itch. When she scratched her scalp, it broke out in bleeding sores. Most days she covered her hair and scalp with a scarf, but that didn't help the damage.

Davis prayed for a solution to her problem. She later said that the answer came to her in a dream: "A big black man appeared to me and told me what to mix up for my hair. Some of the remedy was grown in Africa, but I sent for it, mixed it, put it on my scalp and in a few weeks my hair was coming in faster than it had ever fallen out."

The earliest known photos of Walker displayed before and after effects of her product.

The solution that Davis found not only helped her hair, it also made her the first African-American female millionaire. As Madam C. J. Walker, she developed her idea into an entire line of beauty products. The Walker System was a technique that used special products and hot combs to smooth and straighten hair. The line also included shampoo, hair oil, perfume, toothpaste, soap, powder, and makeup—all designed especially for African-American women. The company would

Madam C. J. Walker (front in tiered dress) posed with her sales agents and employees at the first convention of her company.

eventually employ more than 3,000 African-American men and women. It would become the largest black-owned business in the United States of its time.

Madam C. J. Walker didn't just use her business to help herself. She taught other black women how to treat hair and go into business for themselves by selling her products. At the time the only jobs open to most

African-American women were as household servants or laundresses. Working as Walker agents allowed thousands of African-American women to earn far more than they ever could at those jobs. As business owners, it also gave them a degree of independence that they hadn't had before.

Walker never stopped working hard. As a nationally known business leader, she would influence and be influenced by black artists, educators, poets, and politicians. She would generously contribute part of her wealth to help African-Americans gain racial equality and to support other causes. By personal example, Walker brought hope and optimism to many black women and furthered the cause of civil rights.

After the Civil War many former slaves stayed on farms and plantations as sharecroppers.

Chapter Two

HUMBLE

BEGINNINGS

Sarah Breedlove was born December 23, 1867, in a one-room shack at Grand View, a small cotton plantation in Delta, Louisiana. The future Madam C. J. Walker was the fifth child of Owen and Minerva Breedlove. She was the first one not to be born a slave.

The Civil War had ended just two years before Sarah's birth. Her parents had been slaves at Grand View, which was owned by the Burney family. When the war ended and the 13th Amendment to the U.S. Constitution freed the slaves, the Breedlove family stayed at the plantation. Like many former slaves,

Sarah Breedlove lived with her family in a cabin on the Burney plantation.

Sarah's parents had no education that would allow them to get better jobs. Where they once picked cotton as slaves, they now picked cotton as sharecroppers. They didn't own the land they farmed. Instead, they bought seeds and farming supplies from the landowner, and took a share of the profits when the crops were sold. Some years the fields produced abundant cotton crops. Other years crops failed from drought, disease, or insects.

Two years after Sarah was born the plantation produced a bumper cotton crop. Sarah's parents received about a penny for each pound of cotton that they raised. The money was enough to feed their family as well as pay the $100 fee for their marriage. Before the end of slavery, laws in the South forbade African-Americans from marrying. By the time they were finally able to legally marry in 1869, Owen and Minerva had six children. The oldest was 15-year-old Louvenia and the youngest was baby Solomon, just 2 months old.

From the beginning Sarah's life was one of endless hard work. She helped prepare meals for the family, worked in the garden, and fed the chickens. She and her older siblings spent the rest of the day picking cotton in the fields with their parents. Minerva also took in laundry from white families. On Saturdays Sarah and her sister Louvenia helped their mother scrub clothes outdoors in big wooden tubs. Together they earned about a dollar a week.

Sarah and her family faced other problems besides poverty. In the years after the war, the South was rebuilding and healing from the scars of hard-fought battles. Many white southerners didn't like African-Americans being free, and racial tension grew.

The South was in bad shape after the war. The South had been the site of most of the war's battles. Fields, plantations, and sometimes entire cities and towns had been burned. Train tracks were torn up and roads were rutted. Yet the Breedloves and other former slaves had hopes for better lives. When the war ended, the federal government stepped in to help the South rebuild in a program called Reconstruction.

Many of the new laws passed in the South benefited African-Americans. The 15th Amendment gave African-American men the right to vote in 1870. At the time no women were allowed to vote. It also became legal for black children to attend school. The Breedloves believed that through education, Sarah and their other children could have a better life. An intelligent child, Sarah looked forward to starting school.

LIFE DURING WARTIME

The town of Delta, Louisiana, suffered a great deal of damage during the Civil War. Grand View plantation was across the Mississippi River from the city of Vicksburg, Mississippi. Because it was an important river port, Vicksburg was a prime target for Union forces.

Union General Ulysses S. Grant's soldiers laid siege to the town in May 1863. They blocked anyone from entering or leaving. No food or other supplies were able to pass through the blockade. Union troops bombed the city with cannonballs day and night. The starving residents of the city, both black and white, took refuge in cellars and in caves near the town and ate rats to survive. Confederate Lieutenant General John Pemberton surrendered the city to the Union Army on July 4.

Like many other slaves and owners, the Breedloves and the Burneys fled the battle in July. When the fighting ended, Vicksburg was in ruins. The Breedloves returned to Grand View. It was now a refugee camp for people whose homes had been destroyed in the battle and siege. Thousands of homeless African-Americans lived in horribly crowded conditions at Grand View until they could resettle somewhere else.

But there was a difference between passing laws and enforcing them. When African-American men arrived at polling places to cast their votes, they often found that they were required to pay a tax or prove that they could read before they were allowed to vote. White men were not required to pay the tax or be literate. Many white southerners also tried to stop black children from attending school. Some burned down schools that black children attended and even killed teachers and students.

The Breedloves needed every child, even the youngest ones, to work to help support the family. Sarah received some education at Sunday school classes at the family's church. She learned the alphabet and the basics of reading. But her formal schooling only amounted to about three months. Seven-year-old Sarah's dream of going to school slipped even further away when a double tragedy struck her family. Yellow fever, tuberculosis, cholera, and other infectious diseases spread rapidly in the hot, humid climate along the Mississippi River. Minerva and later Owen came down with a serious illness, perhaps cholera. By 1875 both

Members of the Ku Klux Klan abused and murdered African-Americans.

had died. Their orphaned children ranged in age from 21-year-old Louvenia to 6-year-old Solomon.

Little is known about how and exactly when Sarah's parents died. Few official records were kept for African-Americans at the time. Sarah never spoke publicly about what happened to them except to say,

"I had little or no opportunity when I started out in life, having been left an orphan and being without mother or father since I was seven years of age."

Despite their hard work, the children found it difficult to make a living. Sarah's three older brothers—Alex, Owen Jr., and James—left to find work in the city of Vicksburg, just across the Mississippi River. Louvenia married a man named Jesse Powell and Sarah and Solomon went to live with them. Three years later, in 1878, the family experienced another blow when the cotton crop failed. Now they had no income, and there was no other work they could do to earn money.

In addition, violence against blacks was increasing. That year more than 70 African-Americans near Delta were murdered, mostly by hanging. The family packed up their few belongings and crossed the river to Vicksburg, Mississippi. They hoped life would be better there.

Life at a Glance

NAME AT BIRTH:	Sarah Breedlove
DATE OF BIRTH:	December 23, 1867
BIRTHPLACE:	Grand View plantation, Delta, Louisiana
FATHER:	Owen Breedlove (1828?–1875)
MOTHER:	Minerva Breedlove (1828?–1873)
EDUCATION:	Self-educated and night classes
FIRST SPOUSE:	Moses McWilliams (?–1887)
DATE OF MARRIAGE:	1882
CHILDREN:	Lelia McWilliams Robinson (1885–1931)
SECOND SPOUSE:	John Davis
DATE OF MARRIAGE:	1894
THIRD SPOUSE:	Charles Joseph "C.J." Walker
DATE OF MARRIAGE:	1906
DATE OF DEATH:	May 25, 1919
PLACE OF BURIAL:	Woodlawn Cemetery, New York City

Washing clothes by hand was hard work. Laundry had to be boiled and scrubbed.

Chapter Three

VICKSBURG

LAUNDRESS

Sarah Breedlove had hoped the move to
Vicksburg would mean a better life. That
didn't happen. Even though Sarah worked six days
a week as a washerwoman, her sister's husband
Jesse Powell considered her a burden. Sarah
complained that Jesse was mean and cruel. Sarah
wished she were old enough to find her own place.
When she was 14, she found a way to do that.
She married a man named Moses McWilliams.
He worked as a laborer at whatever jobs he could
find. Sarah never said she was in love with him.
She probably married him to get away from Jesse.

After it was washed, laundry was hung on a clothesline to dry.

"I married at the age of 14," she later said in a matter-of-fact way, "in order to get a home of my own."

In 1885 17-year-old Sarah gave birth to a baby girl, Lelia. Sarah may not have been in love with Moses, but she was thrilled with her baby daughter. She dreamed of having enough money to send Lelia to school and give her all the things she had never had.

LIFE AS A LAUNDRESS

From the time she was a small child, Sarah earned money by washing clothes for several white families. Few jobs, other than picking cotton, were worse than doing laundry in the late 1800s. Even the poorest white women sent out their laundry if they could afford it.

Laundry was a chore that lasted several days. It began on Monday when Sarah would pick up the dirty laundry from the families' homes and carry it back to her own house. She would either carry huge baskets of laundry on her head or use a pushcart for especially large loads.

There were no washing machines or dryers in those days. First Sarah had to boil water in iron pots. Then she would pour the water into wooden washtubs, add harsh lye soap, and soak the dirty clothes, towels, sheets, and tablecloths in the boiling, soapy water. To remove stains, Sarah scrubbed the laundry on a washboard, a wooden frame that held a sheet of tin with ridges. She had to be careful not to scrape her knuckles on the sharp ridges.

Sarah used wooden paddles to remove the heavy, wet laundry from the tubs. She hung it on clotheslines to dry. Then she heated heavy flatirons on her stove to smooth out the wrinkles in bedding, tablecloths, and clothes. She often ironed late into the night. All the laundry had to be washed, ironed, folded, and delivered by Saturday. When she was finished, she returned the clean, folded laundry by the same method she used to pick it up. Sunday was her only day off. The next morning, the process would start all over again.

Life for the next two years was good for Sarah and
Moses. The cotton crop was plentiful, providing most
of the residents of Vicksburg more money for clothes,
shoes, and other goods. But just as life was getting
better for Sarah, her husband died. Historians don't
know for sure what happened to Moses. There were
rumors that he was murdered. Some believe he died in
an accident.

After her husband's death, Sarah didn't know what
to do. She no longer had the support of her three older
brothers. Reconstruction ended in 1877, and the federal
soldiers who were stationed in the South to protect
African-Americans went back north. Her brother Alex
had enough of the prejudice and violence toward
African-Americans. He decided to leave Mississippi
for Kansas in 1882. Many African-Americans were
moving there. They sometimes founded towns that were
made up entirely of black residents. People said that
land there was cheap, black men could vote, and white
people left the African-Americans alone. About 25,000
African-Americans left the South for Kansas in what
became known as the Black Exodus.

Many African-Americans moved to Kansas in search of a better life.

Alex boarded a steamboat sailing to St. Louis, Missouri. From there he planned to travel to Kansas. His brothers Owen Jr. and James followed him. But instead of going on to Kansas, the brothers found that they liked St. Louis and decided to stay there.

Sarah couldn't afford to live on her own and support Lelia. She was determined not to go back to Jesse and Louvenia's house. She decided to follow her brothers to St. Louis.

Men could find work downtown near the river in St. Louis, Missouri.

Chapter Four

A NEW START
IN ST. LOUIS

When 21-year-old Sarah and 3-year-old Lelia arrived in St. Louis early in 1889, they found a city that was very different from their old hometown. Vicksburg's economy was dependent on farming. In contrast, St. Louis was a factory town. Many downtown buildings were built of stone, not wood. Even the air was different. It smelled bad because of the soot and smoke belching into the air from the city's factories.

Owen Jr. had moved to New Mexico in 1883, but Sarah discovered that Alex, James, and her youngest brother, Solomon, were doing well in

St. Louis. They had opened their own barbershop, and business was good. Sarah hoped to find a better-paying job working in a factory or as a domestic servant for a wealthy white family. But white immigrants from Europe usually filled those jobs. Sarah found a place to live and began working six days a week as a laundress again.

As a single mother, Sarah could only afford to live in boardinghouses in violent neighborhoods filled with bars and pool halls. She and Lelia moved often, sometimes staying with one of her brothers when money was especially tight. Sarah enjoyed the company of her brothers and their families. She was especially close to her oldest brother, Alex. She was deeply saddened when he died unexpectedly in 1893.

Besides her family, Sarah had other people to turn to for help. Many of them were members of her church, St. Paul African Methodist Episcopal (AME). Some church members had attended college in the North and were teachers, doctors, or lawyers. Others owned their own businesses. The middle-class women in her church

The orphanage Lelia attended continues to serve children as the Annie Malone Children and Family Services Center.

were especially kind to Sarah. One was Sarah Cohron, a widow who had graduated from Oberlin College in Ohio and later founded the St. Louis Colored Orphans Home. Because Lelia's father was dead, Cohron invited Lelia to live at the orphanage part of the week and attend the local elementary school.

Sarah was happy that her daughter would have the education that she had been denied. But she wanted more for Lelia. Even though she only earned between $4 and $12 each week, she began saving money for Lelia to attend college.

Still, it was difficult for a single woman to improve her life. Sarah later said about those days: "I was at my wash-tubs one morning with a heavy wash before me. As I bent over the washboard, and looked at my arms buried in soapsuds, I said to myself: 'What are you going to do when you grow old and your back gets stiff? Who is going to take care of your little girl?' This set me to thinking, but with all my thinking I couldn't see how I, a poor washerwoman, was going to better my condition."

Hoping to make a better life for herself and her daughter, Sarah accepted the marriage proposal of a man named John Davis. They married August 11, 1894. But Sarah's hopes of a happy marriage and family life weren't to be. Davis drank heavily and had trouble keeping a job. When he was drunk, he

SUPPORT FROM CHURCH

Sarah looked forward to Sundays, her only day off from work. On that day her life revolved around her church, St. Paul African Methodist Episcopal (AME). Founded in the early 1800s, the AME group of churches had been involved for many years in social and political activities. During the Civil War, church members in the North had worked to abolish slavery. After the war AME churches worked to improve the lives of its members.

At church Sarah met wealthy African-American men and women. Sarah was always neatly dressed, but her clothes were patched and shabby. It must have given her hope to see well-off African-Americans. But even though they were successful, they still weren't accepted in white society. They formed their own organizations, such as social clubs and churches. Although Sarah couldn't join middle-class social clubs, she felt welcome in the church.

As poor as she was, Sarah believed in helping others. She joined St. Paul's missionary society, a group dedicated to helping the needy. One of the first things she did was collect money for a poor black man, his blind sister, and sick wife.

Trolley cars and carriages moved through the streets of St. Louis in the late 1800s.

often was verbally and physically abusive. Sarah
felt trapped—just as she had when she was forced
to live with her sister and brother-in-law as a child.

After nine years of unhappy marriage, Sarah had had enough. She left Davis and went back to using the name Sarah McWilliams.

Possibly because of the stress in her life, Sarah's hair began to fall out shortly after her marriage. She tried many types of products and treatments, but nothing helped. At age 35, she was alone, still working as a laundress, and going bald. Two of her brothers died during that time—James in 1902 and Solomon in 1903. Even Sarah's strong religious faith must have been tested at that point. She prayed every night for a solution. Surprisingly enough, it came through a treatment for her hair and scalp problems.

Sarah McWilliams lived in St. Louis until 1905.

Chapter Five

A STEP
TO A BETTER LIFE

*S*arah McWilliams met African-American
hairdresser Annie Pope-Turnbo in 1902.
Pope-Turnbo had come to St. Louis from Illinois
with a new product, Wonderful Hair Grower.
Pope-Turnbo went door-to-door selling her hair
grower as part of the Poro line of hair-care
products. She told women that the key to a healthy
scalp was to wash their hair regularly. Sarah must
have listened to her advice, although it's not certain
if the Wonderful Hair Grower helped cure Sarah's
dandruff and scalp problems or if better hygiene
and less stress helped her hair grow back.

Selling Poro products introduced Sarah McWilliams to the world of hair care.

What is known is that in 1903, Sarah became a Poro agent and began to sell the Wonderful Hair Grower door-to-door. Sarah discovered that she was a good salesperson. She realized that she could make far more money that way than as a laundress, later telling *The New York Times*, "I was considered a good washerwoman and laundress. I am proud of that fact. At times I also did cooking, but, work as I would, I seldom could make more than $1.50 a day. I got my start by giving myself a start. It is often the best way. I believe in push, and we must push ourselves."

Sarah's new job wasn't the only improvement in her life. She had saved enough money to send 17-year-old Lelia to Knoxville College in Tennessee. She began taking night school classes to improve her reading and writing skills. She also fell in love with Charles Joseph "C. J." Walker, who worked for African-American newspapers in St. Louis.

In 1904 St. Louis hosted the World's Fair. Sarah attended the fair and may have been inspired by its many sights and exhibitions to move beyond St. Louis. The next year she decided the time was right. She left St. Louis for Denver, Colorado. She spent most of the money she had on her train ticket, leaving her with just $1.50 to her name.

Sarah arrived in Denver on July 20, 1905. She traveled there alone. C. J. Walker remained in St. Louis, and Lelia was still going to school in Tennessee. But she did have family in the city—her brother Owen's wife, Lucy Breedlove, and four nieces.

Just as St. Louis was very different from Vicksburg, Denver was a complete change from St. Louis. Instead of the dirty air in St. Louis, the mountain air of Denver was crisp and clean. Denver was a frontier town settled by people who were seeking fortunes in gold, silver, and land. About 10,000 African-Americans lived in Denver, where slavery had never been legal. It was a much better place for blacks than St. Louis. It was easier to join social clubs in Denver than in St. Louis. Clubs in St. Louis welcomed mainly well-to-do, educated, middle-class people. In Denver, everyone was welcome. To Sarah, the city seemed like a good place for an African-American woman to start a new business.

Sarah got a job as a cook in a boardinghouse, earning $30 per month. She also began selling Poro products door-to-door during the hours she wasn't at work. She saved as much money as possible to make her dream come true—her own line of hair-care products.

After just four months in Denver, Sarah had saved enough to quit her cooking job at the boardinghouse.

A 1906 view of downtown Denver and the Rocky Mountains

She took in laundry two days a week and sold Poro products, but her main focus was on developing her hair-care line. She rented a small attic space for a laboratory, where she experimented with mixing ingredients that she thought would help heal and strengthen African-American women's hair. She gave her products such names as Wonderful Hair Grower, Brilliantine, and Glossine. Each product container carried a photo of Sarah and her long, thick hair.

Sarah also built relationships with people who would soon become part of her business. She joined an AME church, women's groups, and social clubs that would help promote her hair products to potential buyers.

Sarah put most of the money she earned back into her business, and she advertised in black newspapers. An ad in 1905 read, "Mrs. McWilliams, formerly of St. Louis, has special rates for a month to demonstrate her ability to grow hair." On the days that she wasn't doing laundry, she sought out potential customers for her hair treatments.

"I began of course in a most modest way," she said later. "I made house-to-house canvasses among people of my race, and after a while I got going pretty well, though I naturally encountered many obstacles and discouragements before I finally met with real success." When she went out to sell, she carried her products in a black case and dressed professionally in a starched blouse and long skirt.

By early December 1905, Sarah had a partner both in business and in life. C. J. Walker moved to Denver

Walker's photo was featured on her most popular product.

and asked Sarah to marry him. They were married at
the home of Sarah's friends B. F. and Delilah Givens
on January 4, 1906. Sarah took her husband's name
as part of her own. She was now known as Madam
C. J. Walker, the name she would use for the rest of
her life. Instead of "Mrs.," Sarah chose to use the title
"Madam" for several reasons. It was similar to the
French word madame, which people associated with

elegance and fashion. She also thought it gave her a sense of dignity and authority.

C. J. Walker knew how to promote and advertise his wife's products. To show that the ads for Wonderful Hair Grower were true, he printed before and after pictures of Madam Walker's hair.

Walker developed a hair care system she called the Madam Walker Hair Culture Method. She often gave free demonstrations of her hair care system. It didn't matter if there was a group of women at a demonstration or only one—all got the full treatment.

Walker began her demonstrations by washing a woman's hair with Vegetable Shampoo. Then she applied her Wonderful Hair Grower to the hair and scalp to treat dandruff and heal sores. The final step in the treatment involved a heated steel comb. Walker first rubbed oil into the hair and then used a hot comb to relax and soften the tight curls.

The more Walker demonstrated her products, the more confidence she gained. She found that she had a talent for entertaining audiences as well

HAIR PRODUCT RIVALS

Annie Pope-Turnbo introduced Madam Walker into the hair care business by treating her hair problems and recruiting her as a saleswoman for Poro products. Walker continued to sell Poro products after she moved to Denver, even as she was developing her own hair care line. But by mid-1906 it appeared that Pope-Turnbo wasn't pleased that Walker was striking out on her own. Pope-Turnbo wrote a letter to a Denver newspaper, *The Statesman*, which frequently carried Walker's advertisements. In it, Pope-Turnbo warned customers against using Walker's products, saying "BEWARE OF IMITATIONS." In response, several of Walker's customers sent a letter to the editor detailing how Walker's products had helped them and adding that they intended to remain loyal Walker customers.

Pope-Turnbo probably felt betrayed by someone she had helped and trusted. Walker, however, saw a business opportunity in a new market and seized it. Pope-Turnbo's business later moved to Chicago, Illinois. It was a successful hair product manufacturer until the 1950s.

as selling. African-American women began flocking to Madam Walker's salon, drawn by her products and outgoing personality.

Two newspapers carried Walker's ads for her mail-order business, inviting people to mail in their orders for hair-care products. As orders poured in, Madam Walker needed help to fill the demand for her products. She hired her four nieces, Anjetta, Thirsapen, Mattie, and Gladis, to work for her.

The success convinced Madam Walker that she needed to expand beyond Denver. She traveled to other towns in Colorado, including Pueblo, Trinidad, and Colorado Springs, to sell her products. Her husband and friends were worried that she was spending more money to promote her business than she was making. Madam Walker, however, proved them wrong. Sales kept increasing.

Lelia McWilliams joined her mother and stepfather in Denver in August 1906. At 21, Lelia had graduated from Knoxville College and had also taken hairdressing classes in St. Louis. She began working for her mother,

Walker's company added makeup and skin care products in later years.

performing hair treatments and helping her cousins fill orders.

That year the Walkers left on a sales trip to nine states. Lelia and her cousins stayed in Denver, barely able to keep up with orders that arrived by mail. Madam C. J. Walker was now earning twice as much as the average white American man. And she was just getting started.

Madam Walker led by example and promised her agents they would improve their lives.

Chapter Six

SPREADING
THE WORD

As Madam Walker and C. J. traveled around the country, they developed a system to introduce customers to their hair products. When they arrived in a town, they visited local churches, especially the Baptist and AME congregations, which would have many African-American members. They also contacted African-American social clubs and organizations. Madam Walker held free demonstrations for the groups and took orders for her hair care supplies. She also recruited new agents to sell her products in their communities, training them to perform the Walker Hair Culture.

Many of the women at the demonstrations had grown up on southern farms. Walker spoke to them in terms they understood. "Do you realize that it is as necessary to cultivate the scalp to grow hair as it is to cultivate the soil to grow a garden?" she often began. "Soil that will grow grass will grow a plant. If the grass is removed and the soil cultivated, the plant will be a very healthy one. The same applies to the scalp." Walker assured them that "every woman who wants hair can have it, no matter how short, how stubby, or what the condition of the scalp may be."

Walker's treatments proved popular wherever she went. She received letters from customers who praised her products. They shared personal stories of how the treatments helped their hair.

Even more important to Walker than improving her customers' appearances was the chance to give them a better life. Just as when she entered the workforce as a child, most jobs except household servants or laundresses were closed to black women. She promised the women she recruited as agents that they would have less backbreaking labor and make more money by selling her products. They would also be working for themselves. Walker later said, "I have made it possible for many colored women to abandon the wash-tub for [a] more pleasant and profitable occupation."

Walker learned something else in her travels around the United States. She realized that Colorado's small African-American population meant that it wasn't the best home for her company. She also needed a more central

HELP FROM A FRIEND

Madam Walker always insisted that she got the idea for her hair care line from a dream she had about Africa. But she may have had some help from another person. Pharmacist Edmund Scholtz, who owned the largest drugstore in Denver, may have stayed for a short time at the boardinghouse where Walker worked. Some historians think she might have asked his opinion about the best ingredients to use in her hair-growing formula. Scholtz may have even analyzed the ingredients in the Poro products she sold and suggested how she could make them better.

But no one knows for sure exactly how Walker formulated her Wonderful Hair Grower. She kept her formula a closely guarded secret. One known ingredient, though, was the chemical sulfur, which is still used in some shampoos. Sulfur can kill the germs that cause skin infections.

location to handle her growing mail-order business. When the Walkers visited Pittsburgh, Pennsylvania, in the summer of 1907, they knew they had found their new location. Like St. Louis, Pittsburgh was a sooty, polluted factory town. But the city also had 16 railroad lines, which made it the perfect place to ship packages throughout the United States. It also had the fifth-largest African-American population in the North.

The Walkers moved to Pittsburgh in 1908, and Madam Walker again started networking with black churches and social clubs. She persuaded community leaders to sign a petition endorsing her products. She also opened a beauty salon. She did well in Pittsburgh. She earned $8,700 in 1909, which in today's dollars would be about $200,000.

Madam Walker and Lelia had another idea to help expand their company. They opened a beauty school in Pittsburgh, Lelia College, to train Walker agents. Lelia moved to Pittsburgh in 1908 to help run the school. Women who successfully completed the Lelia College course received a diploma and were known as

Factories dominated the skyline of Pittsburgh, Pennsylvania.

hair culturists. They were also allowed to sell Walker products and open beauty salons that practiced the Walker method. One Lelia College graduate wrote: "You have opened up a trade for hundreds of colored women to make an honest and profitable living where they make as much in a week as a month's salary would

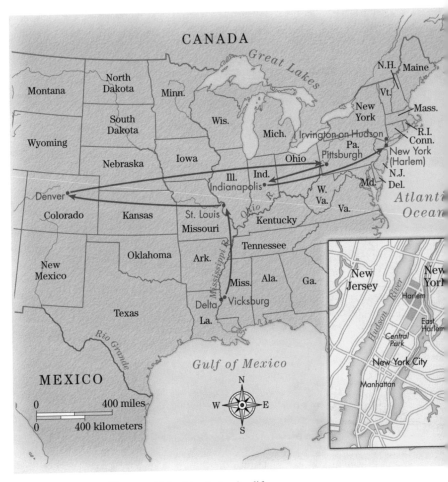

Madam Walker lived in many U.S. cities during her life.

bring from any other position that a colored woman

can secure."

Lelia College graduates began opening hair salons all

over the United States. Madam Walker was soon on the

road again, recruiting agents in Ohio and nearby states. Lelia traveled to eastern states to locate new markets.

Lelia and her mother worked well together, but they didn't always agree. Walker had many hopes and dreams for Lelia, who didn't always appreciate her mother's control. In 1909 Lelia married a man named John Robinson at a courthouse in Washington, Pennsylvania. Walker didn't attend the wedding. She might not have approved of Lelia's choice of a husband, but never commented on her feelings.

By early 1910 Walker decided it was time to move her company's home base again. This time she was looking for land to build a factory where her products could be produced in large quantities. She left Lelia in charge in Pittsburgh and went on the road again.

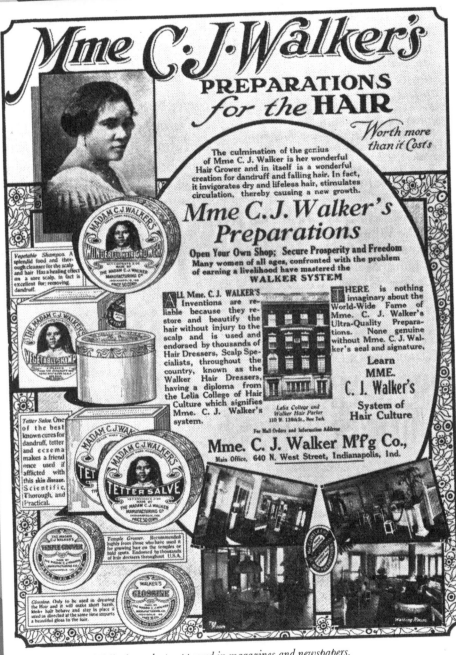

Ads for Madam Walker's products appeared in magazines and newspapers.

chapter Seven

A NEW HOME
AND FACTORY

Madam Walker's search for a location for her factory headquarters took her to several cities, including Indianapolis, Indiana. There she and C. J. stayed at the home of Dr. Joseph Ward, who operated a hospital for African-Americans. Ward and his wife took the Walkers to the Bethel AME Church, as well as many social events. At one of the events, the Walkers met George Knox, who was the publisher of the black newspaper *Indianapolis Freeman*. Knox thought Walker would be an asset to Indianapolis. Many of the 233,000 people living there in 1910 were African-Americans. A greater percentage of blacks lived there than in any other northern city. The city boasted a black middle class of doctors, lawyers, teachers, and other professionals. Many African-Americans owned their own businesses.

Indianapolis was also a major industrial and transportation center. Eight major railroads carried more than 1 million freight cars in and out of the city every year. The city would be an ideal place for Walker's business.

C. J. and Madam Walker bought a brick house for $10,000 on North West Street. They built an addition to the house that would house her factory, laboratory, and beauty salon. Walker continued to pour most of the money she made back into her business. She needed more money to build her factory, so she rented out rooms to boarders in her new home. She also did her own cooking and laundry to save money.

Orders for Walker products poured in as a result of newspaper ads and successful agents across the country. Walker could no longer handle the expanding

Walker on the porch of her Indianapolis home, which was also a salon and factory

business on her own. With her limited education and literacy skills, she needed well-educated people to take leadership roles in her business.

Walker hired two young black lawyers, Robert Brokenburr and Freeman Ransom. Brokenburr set up the Madam C. J. Walker Manufacturing Company as a corporation with capital stock of $10,000. Madam Walker, C. J., and Lelia were the only officers.

Brokenburr later became Walker's assistant manager, but still worked in his law practice part time.

Ransom stayed in Walker's home, giving her legal advice in exchange for room and board. Eventually he became the manufacturing company's general manager—one of the most important people in the company.

Walker met Alice Kelly in Louisville, Kentucky, in 1910. Kelly was a teacher at the Eckstein Norton Institute, a college for African-Americans. Kelly was well educated and spoke French, Latin, and Greek fluently. Walker persuaded Kelly to join her company as the supervisor of the Indianapolis factory in 1912. Walker counted on Kelly to write letters, prepare speeches, and give her advice on etiquette. Walker trusted Kelly so much that she even shared her secret hair-growing formula with her.

One of Kelly's former students, Violet Davis Reynolds, became Walker's private secretary. Two bookkeepers also joined the staff. Walker depended on them for more than business matters. When she came

Walker drove her Model T Ford with passengers niece Anjetta Breedlove (front), Alice Kelly (back right), and bookkeeper Lucy Flint.

across a word she didn't know, she asked them what it meant or had one of them look it up in the dictionary.

After making sure the Indianapolis operation was running smoothly, Madam Walker began traveling again and giving presentations. She still talked about her hair care products, but she also showed photo slides about the achievements of other African-Americans. The slide show made her talks more exciting, and she often spoke to packed houses. Walker also traveled outside the United States. She recruited new Walker agents and set up hair salons on Caribbean islands and in Central America.

But while Walker was enjoying increasing success in business, her personal life wasn't as successful. She and C. J. often argued about money and how the business should be run. They divorced in 1912. Madam Walker would never marry again. Running her business, giving to worthy causes, and working for equality for African-Americans would occupy the rest of her life.

Walker's company had more than 20,000 trained agents by 1917. In August of that year, about 200 of them traveled to Philadelphia, Pennsylvania, to attend the first convention of the Madam C. J. Walker Hair Culturists Union of America. Walker spoke to the group about her company and her path to success, telling them, "There is no royal flower-strewn road to success, and if there is, I have not found it, for what success I have obtained is the result of many sleepless nights and real hard work."

She was earning record amounts of money each year. When a reporter from *The New York Age* asked about her income, she replied: "Well, until recently it gave me great pleasure to tell in my lectures the amount of money I made yearly, thinking it would inspire my hearers. But I found that for so doing some looked upon me as a boastful person who wanted to 'blow my own horn.'"

THE END OF A MARRIAGE

C. J. Walker was the first man Madam Walker had married for love, rather than convenience. But it still wasn't enough to keep them together. Their marriage lasted only seven years. Part of the reason for their split may have been Madam Walker's success. While most African-American women worked to help support their families, husbands were usually the primary breadwinners. C. J. did try to start a business of his own, developing two types of medical tonics. He sold the bottles of Walker's Sore Wash and Walker's Sure Cure Blood and Rheumatic Cure for $1 each. Unlike Madam Walker's products, however, there was no evidence that his products worked, and his business failed.

Madam Walker's daughter, Lelia, also was unlucky in love. She and John Robinson separated after less than a year of marriage, and divorced four years later. She married twice more, but both of those marriages also ended in divorce.

Booker T. Washington's Tuskegee Institute is now Tuskegee University.

chapter Eight

EARNING

RESPECT

As she developed and expanded her business, Madam Walker met many well known and influential African-Americans. Most offered her their support and friendship. But there was one very important member of the African-American community whose respect she had to work long and hard to earn. His name was Booker T. Washington.

Washington was born a slave in Virginia in 1856. After the Civil War his family moved to West Virginia, where he was able to attend school. At age 16 he enrolled in a college for black students. He

SHARING THE WEALTH

Madam Walker's business was doing well and making a good profit, but she didn't keep all the money for herself. She was generous and gave to causes she felt were important. One cause she believed in was education for young African-Americans. She was determined to help them get the formal education she had never had.

Walker met African-American teacher Mary McLeod Bethune at a National Association of Colored Women's conference in 1912. Bethune had founded the Daytona Literary and Industrial Training Institute for Negro Girls in Florida in 1904. The school is now Bethune-Cookman University. Bethune had just five students when she opened the Daytona Beach school. In two years that number had increased to 250. Walker helped raise money for the school and, in 1916, started a course there in hair culture. Bethune and Walker admired each other and became lifelong friends.

Mary McLeod Bethune and her students in 1905

worked as a janitor to pay his way through school and eventually became a teacher. He moved to Tuskegee, Alabama, in 1881 to be the principal of a new school for black students. By the early 1900s Washington had built the Tuskegee Normal and Industrial Institute into a college that trained African-American students to become teachers, farmers, and skilled workers.

In 1910, when Madam Walker was planning to build a factory in Indianapolis, she had an idea to help finance it. She wanted to create a corporation that could issue stock and persuade 100 African-American men and women to invest $50,000 in her business. If the factory was successful, the investors would share the profits.

Walker wanted to keep the stock within the black community. She was afraid that white-owned companies would want to take over her business. They would "want me to sell out my right to them," she said, "which I refuse to do."

Alice Kelly and the Reverend Charles Parrish, president of the Eckstein Norton Institute in Kentucky, supported her idea. They told her to ask Booker T. Washington for help. Walker wrote to Washington, seeking both financial support and advice. But Washington's reply wasn't the news she hoped for.

"My dear Madam," he wrote. "My time and attention are almost wholly occupied with the work of this institution and I do not feel that I can possibly undertake other responsibilities. I hope very much you may be successful in organizing the stock company and that you may be successful in placing upon the market your preparation."

Walker's plan to sell stock in her company didn't work, but she still was able to build the factory in Indianapolis on her own. Even though Washington had refused to help her, she still looked up to him. She agreed with his ideas that African-Americans needed education and training in order to succeed. Washington and Walker both believed that black people should work hard and lead moral lives in order to develop respect for themselves, as well as earn it from others.

Walker's 1927 Indianapolis headquarters would become the Madame Walker Theatre Center, which is home to a variety of programs.

Walker was determined to win Washington's respect for her accomplishments. But that wasn't an easy task.

Hair treatment for black women was a controversial idea. Many black women were uncomfortable with their tightly curled hair and tried to straighten it. Some white-owned cosmetic companies sold products that used harsh chemicals to straighten black women's hair. Washington believed the companies were taking advantage of African-American women. He also said they tried to force white standards of beauty on black women.

Walker wanted to convince Washington that her products weren't meant to make black women look like white women. She wanted him to understand that she was helping African-American women and that she and Washington shared the same goals. Walker knew that earning Washington's approval would benefit her and her business.

In January 1912 Washington was holding the Negro Farmers' Conference at the Tuskegee Institute. Walker wrote to Washington requesting permission to speak to the conference attendees and sell her products on campus. He refused. But Walker went to the conference anyway. She again asked Washington to let her tell her story. He reluctantly allowed her to speak for 10 minutes at a meeting before the conference started.

Washington (seated, second from left) with members of the National Negro Business League executive committee

Eight months later Walker was again at a conference led by Washington—the annual convention of the National Negro Business League in Chicago. Washington had founded the organization in 1900. At these conventions league members shared their ideas and success stories. Walker attended the conference with her friend George Knox, the newspaper publisher. At one point Washington asked for comments from the audience. Knox stood up, introduced Walker, and asked that she be allowed to speak for a few minutes. Washington ignored Knox's request and called on another delegate to speak. Walker knew she would have to try another tactic.

On the last day of the conference, Walker's patience was gone. She stood up and boldly said to Washington, "Surely you are not going to shut the door in my face." With the audience's attention fixed on her, she added: "I feel that I am in a business that is a credit to the womanhood of our race. I went into a business that is despised, that is criticized and talked about by everybody—the business of growing hair. They did not believe such a thing could be done, but I have proven beyond the question of a doubt that I do grow hair!"

The audience laughed and applauded. Walker then made one of her most famous speeches: "I am a woman that came from the cotton fields of the South. I was promoted from there to the wash-tub. Then I was promoted to the cook kitchen, and from there I promoted myself into the business of manufacturing hair goods and preparations."

Walker (seated, third from right) with sales agents

Although interrupted often by the crowd's applause, she continued: "I am not ashamed of my past. I am not ashamed of my humble beginning. Don't think because you have to go down in the wash-tub that you are any less of a lady! Everybody told me I was making a mistake by going into this business, but I know how to grow hair as well as I know how to grow cotton. ... I have built my own factory on my own ground."

Walker and Washington (holding hat) at the dedication of the Indianapolis YMCA

She told the audience that her business was earning $1,500 a month and that she planned to be making double that amount in a year's time. She said her dream was to use her money to help others and to build a Tuskegee Institute in Africa. Washington said nothing and called on the next speaker. But Walker apparently made an impression on him.

The new Indianapolis YMCA was dedicated in July 1913, and Washington was to be the keynote speaker. Walker had contributed $1,000 to the new building. That was an enormous sum for the time and the largest donation by any member of the African-American community, man or woman. Headlines of black newspapers around the country praising her goodwill would help Walker become known as "America's best-known hair culturist."

Walker invited Washington to stay at her house in Indianapolis, and he accepted. In his speech at the dedication ceremony, Washington praised Walker for her large donation to the building. He then asked her to speak at the next annual convention of the National Negro Business League, which was being held in Philadelphia a few weeks later.

At the convention Washington introduced Walker to the audience. In her speech Walker told the crowd that she had indeed made good on her plan to double her income each month. She also talked about her struggles to gain acceptance, saying, "Now in the so-called higher walks of life, many were prone to look down upon 'hair dressers' as they called us. They didn't have a very high opinion of our calling, so I had to go down and dignify this work, so much that many of the best women of our race are now engaged in this line of business, and many of them are now in my employ."

After Walker finished speaking, Washington joined her at the podium, thanking her for her speech and all she had done for their race. He invited Walker to visit Tuskegee Institute in February 1914. At the college Walker spoke to the students and donated money for scholarships, including one for a young man from Africa. She hoped that the student would one day help her achieve her dream of building an industrial school in Africa.

Walker hoped that her new friendship with Washington would persuade him to add hairdressing to the courses offered at the institute. She even offered to pay for a small building on the campus. Washington turned her down, saying that the school's board members weren't ready to add a hairdressing

Walker was a strong supporter of Tuskegee Institute.

program. But Washington continued his public support of Walker, again inviting her to speak at the 1914 convention. He also approved a resolution declaring Walker "the foremost business woman of our race."

When Washington died unexpectedly of heart disease in November 1915, Walker shared how she felt about him: "I have never lost anyone, not even one of my own family that I regret more than I do the loss of this great and good man for he is not only a loss to his immediate relations and friends but to the Race and the world."

Walker fought hard for racial equality.

chapter nine

FACING

DISCRIMINATION

Madam Walker worked hard promoting her business, but she still found time to have fun. One of her favorite pastimes was going to see the silent movies at the Isis Theatre in downtown Indianapolis. One Saturday in 1915, Walker arrived at the movie theater and paid the usual dime admission. The ticket agent pushed the coin back, telling her that admission for blacks had gone up to 25 cents. It was still a dime for white people. Walker was angry about being discriminated against on the basis of her race. She told her attorney, Freeman Ransom, to sue the theater for

$100. There's no record of how the case turned out, but it showed Walker was willing to use her money and influence to fight for racial equality.

After Reconstruction ended, most southern states and cities passed laws that made segregation legal. Blacks and whites sat in separate areas of trains, buses, and restaurants. They had separate restrooms and drinking fountains. And, as Walker's experience in the movie theater showed, racial discrimination wasn't limited just to the South.

Many African-Americans didn't agree on how to fight for equal rights in the early 1900s. A group headed by Booker T. Washington thought blacks should lead by example instead of staging protests. Washington reasoned that blacks would gain greater acceptance in society by becoming educated and working hard. Another group, led by author W. E. B. DuBois, said African-Americans had to fight discrimination with lawsuits and public protests.

Walker didn't completely agree with either Washington or DuBois, although they both had done

W. E. B. DuBois was an educator, journalist, author, and civil rights activist.

great things to help black people. She wanted to
support African-American causes without siding with a
particular leader or group.

But as racial discrimination increased, Walker
realized that protests were an effective way to fight
back. Racists were threatening African-Americans

throughout the country. The Ku Klux Klan was a racist group of white people that wanted to stay in power over blacks, Jews, Catholics, and others that they thought of as inferior. Especially in the South, Klan members threatened African-Americans and committed acts of violence against them. This violence included beatings and lynchings. More than 3,000 people were lynched from 1885 to 1917, three-quarters of whom were African-Americans.

Race riots erupted in both the North and South. One of the worst occurred in East St. Louis, Illinois, in July 1917. A mob of angry white people killed dozens of blacks. Nine white people also died. In black neighborhoods, 16 blocks of houses were burned. Frightened for their safety, about 6,000 African-Americans left the city.

When Madam Walker heard about the riots, she knew the time had come for her to take a stand. The National Association for the Advancement of Colored People (NAACP) was organizing a march to protest the riots and all forms of mob violence. Walker joined

Protesters marched in New York City to demonstrate against the 1917 race riots.

the committee that planned the march. Thousands
of African-American men, women, and children
marched silently down Fifth Avenue in New York City
on July 28, 1917. Thousands of people lined the streets
to watch. The marchers carried signs and banners that
asked for equality and an end to the violence. The
protesters were also upset because African-American

soldiers fighting battles in World War I weren't being treated equally with white soldiers. They asked government leaders, from U.S. President Woodrow Wilson on down, to join their cause.

Four days after the march, Walker and other black leaders took a train to Washington, D.C., to meet with Wilson. He had agreed to meet with them, but when they arrived at the White House, they were told that the president had another appointment. They left a petition for Wilson, which had been signed by 16 well-known African-Americans, including Walker, DuBois, and author and composer James Weldon Johnson.

The petition stated that 36 percent of eligible black men had joined the Army and fought in the war, compared to 25 percent of eligible white men. It asked the president to use his power to help prevent future riots and lynchings. A month later Wilson agreed to a brief meeting with Robert Russa Moton, who had been principal of Tuskegee Institute since Booker T. Washington's death. But still Wilson refused to speak publicly about the issue.

People crowded the sidewalks to view the damage in East St. Louis after the riots.

Furious with the president's silence, Walker shared her feelings with her hair care agents at their convention in August 1917. She urged the agents to speak out about the issue when they returned to their hometowns. She told them, "We should protest until the American sense of justice is so aroused that such affairs as the East St. Louis riot be forever impossible."

Inspired by Walker's words, the agents sent a telegram to Wilson urging him to support laws that would help put a stop to riots and murders. The following month Walker was elected vice president of the National Equal Rights League (NERL), a group headed by William Trotter. Walker worked with her good friend, journalist Ida Wells-Barnett, on an anti-lynching campaign and on ways to end segregation and racial inequality.

World War I ended in November 1918 when the Allied Powers, including the United States, defeated the Central Powers of Austria-Hungary, Germany, and others. The Allies planned to meet in Paris, France, in 1919 to draft a peace treaty between the two sides. The NERL decided to hold its own peace conference in Paris at the same time. League members planned to discuss how to protect the rights of the returning African-American soldiers. Both Walker and Wells-Barnett were invited to be delegates.

Walker's general manager, Freeman Ransom, wasn't happy about Walker's plans. He believed that the NERL was too radical. He wrote Walker and warned her not to go to Paris. "You must always bear in mind

IDA WELLS-BARNETT

Ida Wells-Barnett was born a slave in Holly Springs, Mississippi, in 1862. After the Civil War her father helped start a school for black students, which is now called Rust College. Ida attended the school until her parents died of yellow fever when she was 16. To support her siblings, she got a job as a teacher.

At age 20 she moved her family to Memphis, Tennessee, and became a journalist. In 1884 she was removed from a train in Tennessee after refusing to give up her seat to a white man. She sued the railroad. She won her case in a lower court, but the state Supreme Court overturned the victory. After three of her friends were lynched in Memphis in 1892, she began a campaign to end lynching. She moved to Chicago in 1894, became editor of one of the city's black newspapers, and kept working to end racial discrimination and gain the right to vote for all American women, black and white. In 1930 she ran for a seat in the Illinois state legislature, but wasn't elected. She died in 1931 at age 69.

Inspiring Stories

that you have a large business, whereas the others who are going have nothing. There are many ways in which your business can be circumscribed [lose power] and hampered so as to practically put you out of business."

Walker replied to Ransom in a February 4, 1919, letter: "Your arguments have been passionate indeed against my participation in the Paris peace conference meetings planned by Mr. Trotter. I agree it is best to try to change a system from within, but I thought Mrs. Ida Wells-Barnett and myself would have represented our race well in the talks overseas. My great fear is that the world will finally forge its peace treaties, but Negroes will be left out entirely."

Ransom also wasn't pleased that Walker was part of the International League of Darker Peoples. He said she shouldn't be involved with the people who were part of it. His warning came too late, however. Military spies were already watching Walker because of her association with the group. Her passport application was denied, along with those of most of the other group members. Eventually, Walker listened to

Walker and others met in 1919 with Japanese publisher S. Kuriowa (center), a delegate to the Paris peace conference.

Ransom's warnings and resigned from the International League of Darker Peoples.

In Paris, the Versailles Treaty officially ended World War I. But it didn't mention the rights of African-American soldiers. Racial prejudice would keep growing in the United States for many years to come. The country did little to end the discrimination and violence until another generation of black leaders launched the civil rights movement in the 1960s.

Lelia Walker Robinson, who changed her name to A'Lelia, was an important patron of the arts.

Chapter Ten

LATER

YEARS

The Harlem section of New York City was the center of African-American creativity in the 1920s and 1930s. During what became known as the Harlem Renaissance, black writers and artists had opportunities to share their works with the world. Both black and white people came to hear great jazz musicians perform at Harlem's famous Apollo Theater and other clubs. The area was also a popular place for black doctors, lawyers, and other professionals to live and work.

Walker's daughter, Lelia, had moved to Harlem from Indianapolis in 1913 to set up a branch of Lelia College and a Walker hair salon. Madam Walker bought a townhouse in Harlem, which Lelia spared no expense in remodeling into the college and hair salon. Walker usually indulged Lelia in whatever she wanted, but this time the amount of money Lelia was spending had her concerned. Walker's general manager, Freeman Ransom, was even more worried.

Madam Walker went to New York to check on Lelia's plans. She was amazed at what she saw. The hair salon was elegantly decorated in soft gray, royal blue, and white marble. "The decorators said that of all the work they had done here in that line there is nothing equal to it, not even on Fifth Avenue," she wrote to Ransom. Walker was proud that Lelia's salon was more beautiful than the exclusive salons of hairdressers such as Elizabeth Arden and Helena Rubinstein, which catered to wealthy white women.

Lelia was eager for her mother to join her in New York, which she did in 1916. Lelia bought the building

Walker's daughter, Lelia, who was very involved in the business, had a manicure at a Walker salon.

next door to the salon and had it remodeled into a single unit. The salon and college were on one side, while the other was a home for Madam Walker, Lelia, and her daughter, Mae. Lelia had adopted Mae in Indianapolis in 1912, when the girl was 13.

Madam Walker became famous in New York for her elegant dinners and parties at her home. The house was filled with expensive furniture and artwork, as well as music. Madam Walker and Lelia owned gold-trimmed musical instruments, including a large organ, a grand piano, and a harp, which Mae learned to play.

Walker liked New York City, but she said she wasn't content to live there. She also considered the townhouse more Lelia's home than hers. In 1916 she bought $4\frac{1}{2}$ acres (1.8 hectares) of land along the Hudson River. She planned to build her dream house there—a 30-room mansion. Her neighbors would include white millionaires such as oil tycoon John D. Rockefeller and railroad owner Jay Gould.

Walker regularly visited the huge house as it was being built. When Ida Wells-Barnett was in New York for a National Equal Rights League convention, Walker took her to the construction site. Wells-Barnett later wrote: "We drove out there almost every day, and I asked her on one occasion what on earth she would do with a thirty-room house. She said, 'I want plenty of

Walker agents attended a national convention at Villa Lewaro.

room in which to entertain my friends. I have worked so hard all of my life that I would like to rest.'"

The white stucco mansion with the Spanish tile roof was completed in June 1918, at a cost of about $250,000. When Lelia invited the famous opera singer Enrico Caruso to visit the house, he said it reminded him of a villa in his home country of Italy. He suggested that Madam Walker call the estate Lewaro. The name came from the first two letters in Lelia's

Villa Lewaro was designated a national historic landmark in 1976.

full name: LElia WAlker RObinson. Walker liked the
idea, and the mansion on the Hudson River became
Villa Lewaro.

Walker hoped to make her home at Villa Lewaro for
many years. But health problems had started to plague
her even before she bought the land for the estate.
While her business was doing well, she never felt like
she could slow down her constant traveling. It wasn't
until her car was almost hit by a freight train that she
agreed to take some time off. But Walker's problems

were caused by more than exhaustion. She was suffering from high blood pressure and the early stages of kidney disease.

On her doctor's recommendation, Walker went to Hot Springs, Arkansas, in November 1916. Health spas were built around the area's natural mineral springs. Walker stayed at one of the spas for three months. She soaked in hot mineral baths and enjoyed relaxing massages. Her health began to improve.

Feeling much better, she went back to expanding her company and supporting organizations that were fighting for African-American equality. But by November 1917 her blood pressure had again skyrocketed. She was diagnosed with nephritis, an incurable kidney disease. Her doctor ordered her to check into a famous sanatorium in Battle Creek, Michigan, run by Dr. John Harvey Kellogg.

At Battle Creek, Walker exercised regularly and ate a vegetarian diet. But she stayed only a few weeks at the sanatorium. Her doctor urged her to retire, but Walker wouldn't hear of it.

Walker spent three months traveling on a sales trip through the Midwest in 1918. She also visited military camps where black soldiers were stationed. She strongly believed that the United States owed a debt to African-American soldiers. When Harlem's 369th Army Regiment returned from World War I, Walker invited them to her villa.

At the beginning of 1919, 51-year-old Walker was again feeling tired. She promised to stay home and get more rest. But by the end of March, she was on the road again. After visiting her factory in Indianapolis, she headed to St. Louis to introduce a new line of skin care products. She also looked forward to attending Easter Sunday services at her old church, St. Paul's AME in St. Louis. But while staying at the home of her old friends C. K. and Jessie Robinson, she was so sick that her hosts insisted on calling a doctor. Walker told Jessie that she knew she didn't have long to live, but wished she had more time. "My desire now is to do more than ever for my race," she said. "I would love to live for them. I've caught the vision. I can see what they need."

MAE WALKER ROBINSON

Fairy Mae Bryant grew up as one of seven children in Noblesville, Indiana. Her father died when she was just 10 years old. During summers and holidays, she often came to Indianapolis to visit her grandmother, a laundress who lived across the alley from the Walkers' home. Fairy Mae probably ran errands for the Walker hair parlor. Madam Walker noticed her beautiful, thick braided hair and hired her to model for the Walker Manufacturing Company's advertisements. As they spent more time with Fairy Mae, both Madam Walker and Lelia became very fond of her.

Fairy Mae was a good student, but her widowed mother couldn't afford to send her to high school. Lelia, who was separated from John Robinson and had no children, asked Fairy Mae's mother for permission to legally adopt her daughter. Both Lelia and Madam Walker promised to pay for Fairy Mae's education, train her to run their company, and allow her to stay in contact with her biological family. Knowing the adoption would open many opportunities to her daughter, Mrs. Bryant agreed. In 1912, 13-year-old Fairy Mae Bryant became Mae Walker Robinson. Mae graduated from high school and college, married twice, and had two children. Her granddaughter, A'Lelia Perry Bundles, later wrote a biography of Madam C. J. Walker.

Graduates of the Walker Beauty School would carry on Walker's legacy.

By Monday, April 28, Madam Walker's kidneys were failing. She wanted to return to Villa Lewaro. A private railroad car took her back to the estate that she loved and had enjoyed for such a short time. Flowers and letters from friends and well-wishers filled the mansion as she rested in bed. Lelia and Mae, who were in Panama, searched for the quickest way to get home, but were delayed by ship schedules. They were several hundred miles from the Louisiana coast when

they received word
of Madam Walker's
death on May 25.

The Associated
Press spread the news
that "the wealthiest
negro woman in the
United States, if not
the entire world" had
died. Thousands of
mourners traveled
to Walker's funeral
at Villa Lewaro
on May 30. Many

Mary McLeod Bethune

important African-Americans paid their last respects to
the woman who had overcome poverty and the cotton
fields to become the first American self-made female
millionaire. Among the speakers at the funeral was
Mary McLeod Bethune. "She has gone," said Bethune,
"but her work still lives and shall live as an inspiration
to not only her race but to the world."

Madam C. J. Walker was buried in Woodlawn Cemetery in the north Bronx, New York City. Lelia survived her mother by just 12 years, dying at age 46 in 1931. Lelia willed Villa Lewaro to the NAACP, which sold it to an organization that used it as a retirement home until the 1980s. It's now a private residence. The Walker Manufacturing Company produced hair products until it was sold in 1986.

Madam Walker's memory is still honored by two historic landmarks: Villa Lewaro and the Madame Walker Theatre Center in Indianapolis. But her real legacy is the chance of a better life that she brought to thousands of African-American women. She also left a hope for racial equality that helped change the world and inspire future generations.

A stamp honoring Walker is part of the postal service's Black Heritage series.

Timeline

1882
Marries Moses
McWilliams

1867
Born December 23 in
Delta, Louisiana

1878
Moves to Vicksburg,
Mississippi, and
lives with her sister
Louvenia

1885
Daughter Lelia is born

1873
Mother, Minerva Breedlove,
dies; father, Owen Breedlove,
dies in 1875

1894
Marries John Davis,
from whom she
would separate
after nine years

1889
Moves with Lelia to
St. Louis, Missouri

1887
Husband Moses
McWilliams dies

1905
Moves to Denver, Colorado;
develops formula for
Wonderful Hair Grower

Timeline

1912
Divorces C. J. Walker; daughter adopts Mae Walker Robinson

1910
Moves to Indianapolis, Indiana; buys a home and builds a factory

1906
Marries C. J. Walker; travels to promote her products and recruit sales agents

1911
Incorporates the Walker Manufacturing Company; donates money to the Indianapolis YMCA for African-Americans

1908
Moves to Pittsburgh, Pennsylvania; opens a hair parlor and Lelia College to train agents

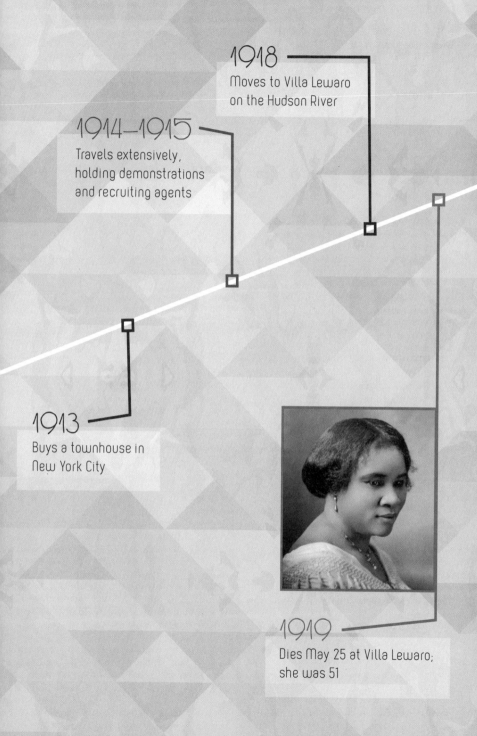

1918
Moves to Villa Lewaro
on the Hudson River

1914–1915
Travels extensively,
holding demonstrations
and recruiting agents

1913
Buys a townhouse in
New York City

1919
Dies May 25 at Villa Lewaro;
she was 51

Glossary

cholera—dangerous disease that causes severe sickness and diarrhea

civil rights—legal rights guaranteed by the U.S. Constitution to every citizen relating to such things as voting and receiving equal treatment

dandruff—scalp condition characterized by itching and shedding flakes of skin

discrimination—unfair treatment of a person or group, often because of race, religion, gender, sexual preference, or age

lynching—putting to death, often by hanging, by mob action and without legal authority

prejudice—hatred or unfair treatment of people who belong to a certain social group, such as a race or religion

radical—extreme compared to what most people think or do

Reconstruction—period following the Civil War, from 1865 to 1877, when the federal government controlled states in the former Confederacy and granted rights to African-Americans

renaissance—time of great revival of art and culture

sanatorium—institution for rest and maintaining or improving health

segregation—the practice of keeping groups of people apart, especially based on race

sharecropper—farmer who works the land in exchange for housing and part of the profits

stock—the value of a company, divided into shares when sold to investors

tuberculosis—disease that affects the lungs and causes fever, cough, and difficulty breathing

yellow fever—illness that can cause high fever, chills, nausea, and liver and kidney failure; liver failure causes the skin to become yellow, giving the disease its name

Further Reading

Arora, Sabina. G., ed. *The Great Migration and the Harlem Renaissance.* New York: Britannica Educational Publishing in association with Rosen Educational Services, 2016.

Braun, Sandra. *Women Inventors Who Changed the World.* New York: Rosen Central, 2012.

Hillery, Louise. *Bold Women in Indiana History.* Missoula, Mont.: Mountain Press Publishing Company, 2016.

Lassieur, Allison. *The Harlem Renaissance: An Interactive History Adventure.* North Mankato, Minn.: Capstone Press, 2014.

Internet Sites

Use FactHound to find Internet sites related to this book. All of the sites on FactHound have been researched by our staff.

Here's all you do:

Visit www.facthound.com

Type in this code: 9780756551650

OTHER BOOKS IN THIS SERIES

source notes

Page 6, line 15: Ayana D. Byrd and Lori L. Tharps. *Hair Story: Untangling the Roots of Black Hair in America.* New York: St. Martin's Griffin, 2014, p. 34.

Page 18, line 1: A'Leilia Perry Bundles. *On Her Own Ground: The Life and Times of Madam C.J. Walker.* New York: Scribner, 2001, p. 34.

Page 22, line 1: Ibid., p. 40.

Page 30, line 7: "Wealthiest Negro Woman's Suburban Mansion." *The New York Times Magazine Section.* 4 Nov. 1917, p.6.

Page 36, line 6: Ibid.

Page 40, line 7: *On Her Own Ground: The Life and Times of Madam C.J. Walker,* p. 83.

Page 40, line 12: "Wealthiest Negro Woman's Suburban Mansion."

Page 43, line 10: *On Her Own Ground: The Life and Times of Madam C.J. Walker,* p. 89.

Page 48, line 3: Ibid., p. 98.

Page 49, line 6: Ibid., p. 154.

Page 51, line 4: Noliwe M. Rooks. *Hair Raising: Beauty, Culture, and African American Women.* New Brunswick, N.J.: Rutgers University Press, 2000, p. 93.

Page 60, line 18: Hugh C. Price. "To Be Equal: Madame Walker Showed Hard Work Pays." *The Muncie Times.* 19 Feb. 1998, p. 10.

Page 61, line 3: *The New York Age.* 2 March 1916, p.1.

Page 65, line 18: Beverly Lowry. *Her Dream of Dreams: The Rise and Triumph of Madam C.J. Walker.* New York: Alfred A. Knopf, 2003, p. 225.

Page 66, line 5: *On Her Own Ground: The Life and Times of Madam C.J. Walker,* p. 101.

Page 70, line 7: Ibid., p. 135.

Page 73, line 9: *Her Dream of Dreams: The Rise and Triumph of Madam C.J. Walker*, p. 264.

Page 73, line 21: *On Her Own Ground: The Life and Times of Madam C.J. Walker*, p. 149.

Page 75, line 4: Virginia C. Drachman. *Enterprising Women: 250 Years of American Business.* Chapel Hill: The University of North Carolina Press, 2002, p. 85.

Page 75, line 7: *On Her Own Ground: The Life and Times of Madam C.J. Walker*, p. 166.

Page 83, line 5: Ibid., p. 212.

Page 84, line 21: Ibid., p. 254.

Page 86, line 6: Tananarive Due. *The Black Rose*. New York: Ballantine Publishing Group, 2000, pp. 354–355.

Page 90, line 13: *On Her Own Ground: The Life and Times of Madam C.J. Walker*, p. 169.

Page 92, line 19: Lorraine Elena Roses and Ruth Elizabeth Randolph, eds. *Harlem's Glory: Black Women Writing*, 1900–1950. Cambridge, Mass.: Harvard University Press, 1996, p., 221.

Page 96, line 19: *On Her Own Ground: The Life and Times of Madam C.J. Walker*, p. 269.

Page 99, line 6: Ibid., p. 275.

Page 99, line 19: Ibid., p. 277.

Select Bibliography

Alexander, Amy. *Fifty Black Women Who Changed America.*
Secaucus, N.J.: Carol Publishing Group, 1999.

Bundles, A'Lelia Perry. "Madam C.J. Walker's Secrets to Success." Biography.com.
24 Feb. 2015. 10 Dec. 2015. http://www.biography.com/news/madam-cj-walker-
biography-facts

Bundles, A'Lelia Perry. *On Her Own Ground: The Life and Times of Madam C.J. Walker.*
New York: Scribner, 2001.

Byrd, Ayana D., and Lori L. Tharps. *Hair Story: Untangling the Roots of Black Hair in
America.* New York: St. Martin's Griffin, 2014.

Drachman, Virginia C. *Enterprising Women: 250 Years of American Business.*
Chapel Hill: The University of North Carolina Press, 2002.

Due, Tananarive. *The Black Rose.* New York: Ballantine Publishing Group, 2000.

James, Edward T., ed. *Notable American Women: A Biographical Dictionary, Vol. III:
1607–1950,* P–Z. Cambridge, Mass.: Belknap Press of Harvard University Press, 1971.

Lommel, Cookie. *Madam C.J. Walker.* Los Angeles: Melrose Square Pub. Co., 1993.

Lowry, Beverly. *Her Dream of Dreams: The Rise and Triumph of Madam C.J. Walker.*
New York: Alfred A. Knopf, 2003.

Madam CJ Walker: The Official Web Site of All Things Related to Madam C.J. Walker.
http://www.madamcjwalker.com/#&panel1-1

"Over 10,000 in Her Employ." *The New York Age.* 2 March 1916.

Peiss, Kathy. *Hope in a Jar: The Making of America's Beauty Culture.*
New York: Metropolitan Books, 1998.

Rooks, Noliwe M. *Hair Raising: Beauty, Culture, and African American Women.*
New Brunswick, N.J.: Rutgers University Press, 1996.

Roses, Lorraine Elena, and Ruth Elizabeth Randolph, eds. *Harlem's Glory: Black Women
Writing, 1900–1950.* Cambridge, Mass.: Harvard University Press, 1996.

Two American Entrepreneurs: Madam C.J. Walker and J.C. Penney. National Park
Service. http://www.nps.gov/nr/twhp/wwwlps/lessons/walker/Walker.htm

"Wealthiest Negress Dead" by The New York Times. *The New York Times.* 26 May 1919.
10 Dec. 2015. http://www.nytimes.com/learning/general/onthisday/bday/1223.html

"Wealthiest Negro Woman's Suburban Mansion." *The New York Times Magazine Section.*
4 Nov. 1917.

Index

advertisements 40, 42, 43, 44, 56, 97
agents 9, 47, 48–49, 50, 53, 56, 60, 83–84

Bethune, Mary McLeod 64, 99
birth 11
Black Exodus 24
Breedlove, Alex (brother) 18, 24–25, 27–28
Breedlove, James (brother) 18, 24, 25, 27–28, 33
Breedlove, Louvenia (sister) 13, 16, 18, 25
Breedlove, Lucy (sister-in-law) 37
Breedlove, Minerva (mother) 11, 13, 16–18
Breedlove, Owen (father) 11, 13, 16–18
Breedlove, Owen, Jr. (brother) 18, 24, 25, 27, 37
Breedlove, Solomon (brother) 13, 16, 18, 27–28, 33
Brokenburr, Robert 57, 58

childhood 13, 17–18
Civil War 11, 13–14, 15, 31
Cohron, Sarah 29
cooking job 36, 38, 70

Davis, John (husband) 30, 32–33
death 99
Delta, Louisiana 11, 15, 18
demonstrations 42, 44, 47–48
Denver, Colorado 37–38, 43
divorce 60, 61
DuBois, W. E. B. 78–79, 82

education 14, 16, 30, 57, 64, 66, 74–75, 78

factory 53, 55, 56, 58, 65, 66, 96

Grand View plantation 11, 15
Grant, Ulysses S. 15

hair 5–7, 33, 35, 39, 42, 48, 67–68
Harlem Renaissance 89
health 94–95, 98

income 18, 61, 72, 73
incorporation 57, 65
Indianapolis, Indiana 55–56, 66, 73, 77, 100
ingredients 6, 39, 49, 58
International League of Darker Peoples 86–87
Isis Theatre 77–78

Johnson, James Weldon 82

Kellogg, John Harvey 95
Kelly, Alice 58, 65–66
Knox, George 55, 69–70
Ku Klux Klan 80

laboratory 39, 56
laundress job 6, 21, 23, 28, 30, 36, 39, 70
Lelia College 50–52, 90, 91
Life at a Glance 19
lynchings 80, 82, 84, 85

Madame Walker Theatre Center 100
Madam Walker Hair Culture Method 7, 42, 47, 51
marriages 21–22, 30, 41, 61
McWilliams, Moses (husband) 21, 22, 24
Moton, Robert Russa 82

National Association for the Advancement of Colored People (NAACP) 80, 100
National Equal Rights League (NERL) 84
National Negro Business League 69–72, 73
New York City, New York 81, 89–90, 92, 100

Parrish, Charles 65–66
peace conference 84, 86
Pemberton, John 15
Pittsburgh, Pennsylvania 50
poll taxes 16
Pope-Turnbo, Annie 35, 43
Poro products 35–37, 38, 39, 43, 49
Powell, Jesse 18, 21, 25
protests 78–80, 80–82, 83

Index cont.

Ransom, Freeman 57, 58, 77, 84, 86, 90
Reconstruction 14, 24, 78
Reynolds, Violet Davis 58
Robinson, John 53, 61, 97
Robinson, Lelia Walker (daughter) 22,
    25, 27, 28, 29–30, 37, 44–45, 50,
    53, 57, 61, 90, 91, 92, 93–94, 97,
    98–99, 100
Robinson, Mae Walker (granddaughter)
    91, 92, 97, 98–99

salesperson job 36–37, 38, 39, 43
sales trips 44, 45, 47–48, 52–53,
    59–60, 96
salons 44, 50, 51, 52, 56, 60, 90, 91
Scholtz, Edmund 49
segregation 78, 84
slavery 11–12, 31, 38, 63
speeches 70–72, 73–74
St. Louis Colored Orphans Home 29
St. Louis, Missouri 25, 27–28, 37, 38, 96
St. Paul African Methodist Episcopal
    (AME) Church 28–29, 31, 96

Trotter, William 84, 86
Tuskegee Normal and Industrial Institute
    65, 68, 72, 74–75, 82

Versailles Treaty 87
Vicksburg, Mississippi 15, 18, 21, 24
Villa Lewaro 92–94, 98, 99, 100

Walker, Charles Joseph "C. J." (husband)
    37, 40–41, 42, 47, 55, 56, 57, 60, 61
Ward, Joseph 55
Washington, Booker T. 63, 65, 66–67,
    68–72, 73, 74–75, 78–79
Wells-Barnett, Ida 84, 85, 86, 92
Wilson, Woodrow 82–83, 83–84
Wonderful Hair Grower 35–36, 39, 42,
    49
World's Fair (1904) 37
World War I 82, 84, 87, 96

YMCA building 73

CRITICAL THINKING USING THE COMMON CORE

1. Madam Walker overcame an early life of poverty to become one of the most successful businesswomen of her time. How did she do this? Support your answer with evidence from the text. (Key Ideas and Details)

2. During Walker's life, racism prevented most African-Americans from getting good educations or well-paying jobs. Is racism still an issue in the United States today? Why or why not? (Integration of Knowledge and Ideas)

3. Walker had a complicated relationship with Booker T. Washington. She worked hard to earn his respect. Why do you think Washington felt the way he did about Walker? What do you think changed his mind? (Integration of Knowledge and Ideas)